Destination Detectives

Spain

North America

Europe

Asia

SPAIN

Africa

South America

Australasia

Paul Mason

Raintree

www.raintreepublishers.co.uk
Visit our website to find out more information about **Raintree** books.

To order:
☎ Phone 44 (0) 1865 888112
▤ Send a fax to 44 (0) 1865 314091
▢ Visit the Raintree Bookshop at **www.raintreepublishers.co.uk** to browse our catalogue and order online.

First published in Great Britain by
Raintree, Halley Court, Jordan Hill,
Oxford OX2 8EJ, part of Harcourt Education.
Raintree is a registered trademark of Harcourt
Education Ltd.

Editorial: Melanie Copland and Lucy Beevor
Design: Victoria Bevan and Kamae Design
Picture Research: Hannah Taylor and Kay Altwegg
Production: Duncan Gilbert

Originated by Dot Gradations
Printed and bound in China
by WKT Company Limited

ISBN 1 844 2140 87
10 09 08 07 06
10 9 8 7 6 5 4 3 2 1

British Library Cataloguing in Publication Data
Mason, Paul
Spain. – (Destination Detectives)
946'.083
A full catalogue record for this book is available from
the British Library.

Acknowledgements
Action Plus pp. 6t (Glyn Kirk), 20–21 (Neil Tingle); Alamy Images
pp. 12–13 (Chris Knapton), 5m, 39 (Dalgleish Images), 17 (Ian
Dagnall), 4 (Loetscher Martin), 22 (Mark Beton), 24–25 (Nicholas
Pitt), pp. 11, 18–19 (Scott Hortop), 34l (Stuart Walker).
Bridgeman Art Library pp. 10–11(Private Collection, Christie's
Images); Corbis pp. 15 (Erik Schaffer; Ecoscene), 8–9 (Patrick
Ward), pp. 5t, 18, 43 (Reuters), 23 (Tim De Waele/Isosport);
Corbis Sygma p. 36 (Landmann Patrick); Food Features p.5; Getty
Images p. 6l (Photodisc); Rex Features pp. 37 (D Maxwell), 40
(Eye Ubiquitous), 41t (Heikki Saukkomaa), 31 (Ilpo Musto), 21
(Nils Jorgensen), 33 (R. G. Williamson), 24 (Ray Tang), 28
(Rick Colls), pp. 5b, 14, 32, 35, 42t (Sipa Press), 29 (The Travel
Library); Robert Harding pp. 30–31 (Digital Vision), 41b (Jean
Brooks), 34r (Michael Busselle), 16 (Michael Jenner); Turespana
pp. 6 br, 9, 12, 26, 27, 38, 42b.

Cover photograph of flamenco costume reproduced with
permission of Getty Images/Photographer's Choice.

Every effort has been made to contact copyright
holders of any material reproduced in this book.
Any omissions will be rectified in subsequent
printings if notice is given to the publishers.

The paper used to print this book comes from
sustainable resources.

Disclaimer
All the Internet addresses (URLs) given in this book were valid at
the time of going to press. However, due to the dynamic nature of
the Internet, some addresses may have changed, or sites may have
changed or ceased to exist since publication. While the author and
publishers regret any inconvenience this may cause readers, no
responsibility for any such changes can be accepted by either
the author or the publishers.

Contents

Any words appearing in the text in bold, **like this,** are explained in the glossary. You can also look out for them in the Word Bank box at the bottom of each page.

Where in the world?

Noisy Spain!

"In Spain I hear so much noise from my window that I can't stand it. In Switzerland it's the lack of noise that drives me crazy."

– American actress Geraldine Chaplin describes the lively atmosphere in Spain (and the quiet one in Switzerland!)

What wakes you up first? Is it the noise of the wind banging the shutters of your window? Or the faraway sound of singing? You sit up in bed and push the shutters open to look outside. Bright sunlight reflects off the white buildings, making you blink. The sea crashes against the shore almost under your nose. Where can you be?

Suddenly a man standing on what looks – from this distance – like a giant skateboard zooms past. He is skidding across the waves, dragged by a giant parachute. It takes a minute of waking up to realize he's actually a kitesurfer.

Kitesurfers are dragged across the waves by huge, brightly coloured kites on the beach at Tarifa.
➤

At that moment, there's a knock on the door. You open the door to a man carrying a tray. On it is a mug of what looks like thick, black chocolate and some stringy doughnuts.

"Breakfast!" he says. "*Chocolate con churros*. I hope the **muezzin** did not wake you. When the wind comes across the Mediterranean from North Africa, the sound of their song calling people to prayer reaches all the way to Spain."

At least you know where you are now: in Spain, at the southernmost point, where it almost touches the African country of Morocco. You're in the town of Tarifa.

Churros are long and thin and made of doughnut dough. People dip them in *chocolate*, a thick drink of melted chocolate.

Spain in Africa
*Spain has two **territories** in North Africa. Ceuta is across the Straits of Gibraltar from Algeciras. Melilla is also on the north coast of Morocco.*

Find out later...
Why are these people covered in tomatoes?

What delicious meal can be made from this weird-looking fish?

Why do dangerous bulls run wild on the streets of Pamplona?

territory area of land

Regions of Spain

Spain fact file:

POPULATION:
39.6 million

AREA:
505,000 square kilometres (194,930 square miles)

RELIGION:
many people are Roman Catholic. There are a large amount of North African Muslims in the south.

LANGUAGE: Spanish

CURRENCY: Euro

TYPE OF GOVERNMENT: democratically elected

In a drawer beside your bed you find a map and photographs left behind by another traveller. This is going to come in handy! He or she left lots of scribbled notes, telling you about the different parts of Spain.

Real Madrid is one of the biggest soccer teams in the world.

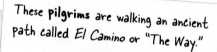

These pilgrims are walking an ancient path called *El Camino* or "The Way."

Catalunya is home to one of Spain's most exciting and beautiful cities — Barcelona. The Catalans have always felt different from other Spaniards, and some even want **independence**.

WORD BANK border imaginary line dividing one country from another
independence when an area governs itself

FRANCE

SPAIN

MOROCCO

The Basque Country – the Basques are tough mountain people. Many of them would like their region to be independent. Some live across the **border** in France, but most Basques live in Spain.

The Balearic Islands – these beautiful Mediterranean islands are a holiday hot spot. Each year, Mallorca alone gets about 3 million visitors!

The Meseta Central – this vast, dry **plateau** lies in the middle of Spain. Mostly it is over 600 metres (656 yards) above sea level. At the Meseta's northern edge is Spain's capital city, Madrid.

The South – this area of Spain is strongly influenced by nearby North Africa. The architecture and the people here are reminders that from AD 711 to 1492, the Moors governed parts of Spain.

The Canary Islands – closer to North Africa than Spain, these Atlantic islands are a favourite holiday destination for European tourists. They are especially popular in winter, when the climate is warmer than Europe's.

Bilbao • San Sebastián
Basque Country
Pyrenees
Ebro River
Catalunya
Barcelona

MEDITERRANEAN SEA

Salamanca
Madrid
Tajo River

Balearic Islands

Valencia

Alicante

Sierra Nevada
▲ Mount Mulhacén
Malaga
Almería
Tarifa
Ceuta
Melilla
Straits of Gibraltar

ATLANTIC OCEAN

PORTUGAL

N
W E
S

0   150 km
0   100 miles

CANARY ISLANDS

Mount Teide ▲

0   150 km
0   100 miles

pilgrim   person making a religious journey
plateau   high area of flat land

7

History

The song that woke you this morning was blown on the wind from North Africa, which is only 15 kilometres (9 miles) away. From the harbour at Tarifa the ferry takes just 35 minutes.

In the past, Moors, or Muslims from North Africa, governed almost the whole of Spain. The **legacy** of the Moors is everywhere. In the south especially, the housing (see photo below), music, and food were all influenced by the Moors. Even the Spanish language contains many words that came originally from Moorish.

MADRID

You are here!

• Granada

Tarifa

N
W • E
S
0   150 km
0   100 miles

The tears of Boabdil

Boabdil was the last Moorish ruler of the beautiful city of Granada. The story goes that Boabdil loved the city so much, he surrendered it to the Christian armies rather than see it destroyed. As he left, he turned for a last sight of Granada and wept.

The Alhambra

One of the most beautiful buildings in Spain is the Alhambra Palace in Granada (see far right). There are three main areas: a Moorish summerhouse, a Moorish palace, and a castle that was built later by Christian forces.

WORD BANK   legacy something handed down through time

Reconquista is the Spanish name for when Christian armies took control of Spain back from the Moors. The Moors were Muslims, and at that time Muslims and Christians fought many battles, right across Spain.

In 1492 the Moors finally lost control of their last Spanish **territory**, around the southern city of Granada. The "reconquest" of Spain from its Muslim rulers was complete.

Castillo de Guzmán, Tarifa

During a **siege** of Tarifa Castle by the Moors in 1292, the 9-year-old son of the Christian Commander, Alonso Pérez de Guzmán, was kidnapped. The Moors would only free him if the castle surrendered. Otherwise he would be killed. Guzmán said he would rather have, "honour without a son, than a son without honour", and threw down his own dagger for the execution.

siege when a building is surrounded by enemy forces who prevent anyone from arriving or leaving

The New World

In 1492, the same year that the "reconquest" ended, the explorer Christopher Columbus reached the shores of North America. These unknown lands were soon called the "New World". Spain quickly took control of large areas of North and South America.

Spain became the richest country in Europe through all the gold and precious items brought back from the New World. Spain's **empire** only broke apart in the 1800s, when many South American countries became **independent**.

Drake attacks!

During the late 1500s, the English sea captain Francis Drake spent most of his time battling the Spanish:

- he **looted** the Spanish city of Nombre de Dios in Central America
- he captured the treasure ship *Cacafuego*
- he held the town of Cartagena, Spain, to ransom
- he helped defeat a Spanish attempt to invade Britain.

Spain's treasures from the New World included gold and silver. They were transported back to Europe in giant "treasure ships". Pirates sometimes attacked the ships!

WORD BANK

civil war war between groups from within the same country. In Spain the civil war was between the Nationalists and the Republicans.

The Spanish Civil War

In 1936, a terrible **civil war** began in Spain. On one side was the elected government. The government had lost control of some areas of the country. In response, a Spanish army officer called General Francisco Franco tried to take over power. War raged in Spain for the next 3 years.

Both sides did terrible things. Many people were killed or tortured during the civil war. It ended in 1939 with a victory for Franco. He stayed in power until his death in 1975. Many Spaniards still remember the war and Franco with great bitterness.

Guernica

The town of Guernica is in the Basque country. It is where the ancient Basque **parliament** used to meet. In 1937 aircraft from Franco's forces bombed Guernica. In just over 3 hours, 1,600 people died and the town was completely destroyed.

The ancient Basque parliament met around the Tree of Guernica for centuries. It still stands today.

looted stolen during a battle or riot

11

Spain's landscape

- In the south, the Guadalquivir gathers waters from behind the coastal mountains.
- In the centre, the Guadiana and Tajo both eventually flow west into Portugal.
- In the north is the Ebro, which is the longest river in Spain.

After you've visited the Castillo de Guzmán and watched the kitesurfers for a while, what else is there to do around here? Plenty! Southern Spain is great for watersports such as sailing, windsurfing, and surfing. Lots of people go cycling or walking in the hills behind the coast.

Spend a couple of hours on a bus and you can reach the mountains of the Sierra Nevada. In springtime it is possible to swim in the warm Mediterranean Sea in the morning, then spend the afternoon snowboarding in the mountains!

The delta of the Guadalquivir River in southern Spain is a nature reserve called the *Coto Doñana*. The reserve is home to eagles and lynx, among other unusual animals.

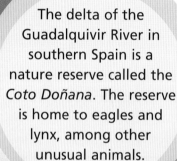

Mountains

To reach Spain's highest mountains, you have to travel far to the north. The Pyrenees form the **border** between Spain and France. In the past invading armies entered Spain through the Pass of Roncesvalles in the Pyrenees. Some were chased back out of Spain the same way.

Further east are the Picos de Europa mountains. These are now a national park. People visit them for hiking, mountain biking, and climbing. The Picos are also home to some amazing wildlife, including vultures, mountain goats, and bears.

Mountain-bike heaven

Spain's many steep mountains have recently seen a big increase in the number of mountain bikers visiting them. In the Picos and the Pyrenees, riders race down specially built trails through the woods. Spain even holds a round of the Downhill World Cup competition at Vigo.

This hiker overlooks Mulhacén, the highest mountain on the Spanish mainland at 3,479 metres (11,414 feet).

Weather

What kind of clothes do you have in your travel bag? Southern Spain is usually warm and dry all year round. The most you need here is a light jacket. This is why the region is a popular holiday destination. The area east of Tarifa called the *Costa del Sol,* "Coast of the Sun," is especially busy. The seaside is lined with high-rise hotels.

Of course, the whole country isn't warm and sunny all the time! Spain has a wide range of climates. If you are planning on exploring, you will need to be able to stay warm and dry.

Wet and windy north

The weather in northern Spain is affected by the Atlantic Ocean. In winter, powerful storms rush in off the sea. The people shut their doors tight, and wrap up warm if they have to go out! In summer the north is warm and usually dry, though the far north-western tip of Spain is the wettest part of the country.

Wind crazy

Tarifa is known mainly for the number of local people driven crazy – at least temporarily – by the high winds that blow through the town almost all the time!

Siesta

Most Spaniards take a long break called a **siesta** *in the middle of the day. The* **siesta** *happens after lunch, when people often take a nap. It's a great way of avoiding the hottest part of the day!*

WORD BANK   arable   farming land where crops are grown

Dry centre

The central plain, or *meseta*, is a very dry region. Some areas are even deserts. In summer the plains can be hot and baked by the sun. In winter they are sometimes freezing cold with an icy wind.

Temperatures around Spain

This table shows the average temperature in some of Spain's cities in January and July:

City	January	July
Alicante	16 °C (60.8 °F)	32 °C (89.6 °F)
Madrid	9 °C (48.2 °F)	31 °C (87.8 °F)
Málaga	17 °C (62.6 °F)	29 °C (84.2 °F)
Mallorca	14 °C (57.2 °F)	29 °C (84.2 °F)
Pontevedra	14 °C (57.2 °F)	25 °C (77 °F)
Seville	15 °C (59 °F)	35 °C (95 °F)

◄ The *Meseta Central* – the high plain in the middle of Spain – has a dry climate. However, the desert can be used for farming, such as this **arable** farm in Andalucia.

siesta   short nap, especially in countries where the sun gets very hot in the afternoon

Food & culture

Food words

bread	*pan*
eggs	*huevos*
rice	*arroz*
fish	*pescados*
soup	*sopa*
shellfish	*mariscos*
meat	*carne*
vegetables	*legumbres*

Now that you have done a bit of exploring, it's probably time for lunch! Spanish people often eat a bigger meal at lunchtime than in the evening. What would a hungry traveller be likely to find on the menu?

The Spanish love fish and seafood. Their fishing fleet is the biggest in Europe. One favourite dish all over Spain is called paella. Paella originally came from Valencia. It contains rice, fish, and some meat (often rabbit or chicken). People also love *zarzuelas*, or fish stews.

Giant paella dishes like this are always brought out at festival time. You can usually buy a little bowl of paella from the cook.

Family nights out

Late nights out in Spain are not only for grown-ups! Often whole families – from grandparents to babies in pushchairs – go out together. They may still be out after midnight, walking and talking to their friends, eating tapas, and sipping drinks.

In the evenings many Spaniards eat small snacks called tapas. Tapas are often called *pinchos* in northern Spain. It's a good name, as they are little portions, or pinches, of food that you can eat quickly. Tapas can be made of almost anything – meat, fish, egg, vegetables, salad, or bread.

If you are feeling a bit too hungry for just tapas, you can ask for *raciones* instead. This is just a bigger helping of the same thing. Someone who is really hungry might eat a *bocadillo*, or sandwich. But most people prefer trying lots of little snacks to one big one!

An evening stroll

After lunch you will need a little Spanish-style **siesta**. All this sight-seeing is tiring! Then it's time to have a look around in the evening.

Spaniards are generally very sociable. They enjoy company, and friends and family are very important to them. One of the things you will notice is how many people go out for a walk in the early evening. They stroll up and down the main street, chatting and greeting their friends. This is called the *paseo*.

Tomatoes

In August the town of Buñol, near Valencia, hosts the *Tomatina* festival. The festival started in 1945, when a fight broke out among people watching a carnival parade. They began throwing tomatoes at each other. The police broke up the fight, but it was such fun that the tomato fight has happened almost every year since!

Today people come from all round the world to take part in *Tomatina*. Over 40,000 kilograms (90,000 pounds) of tomatoes get thrown in just 2 hours. That's the equivalent to the weight of six-and-a-half large elephants!

WORD BANK   patron saint religious figure associated with a place, country, job, or institution

Family and festivals

Family is especially important to most Spanish people. Even grown-up children try to get home for special occasions such as birthdays and Christmas. This often means going back to the town or village where they were born.

People also return to their birthplace for the local festival. Even tiny villages have festivals in honour of their **patron saint**. Two or three days are spent eating and drinking, having fun, and taking part in **processions**.

Elsewhere in Spain there are some very grand festivals. In Seville, as in many parts of Spain, the biggest festival leads up to Easter. In Cádiz, just north-west along the coast from Tarifa, the February carnival (another word for festival) features amazing costumes and music.

The "disguised devils"

The "disguised devils" is a festival where the young boys of the town of Cuenca dress as devils, with large cowbells tied to their waists. They dance at the entrance and inside the church.

Spain's warm weather helps make the evening stroll pleasant.

procession group of people moving in a line as part of a celebration. During festivals processions often end at the church.

Spain's big teams

Spain is home to some of the world's most famous football players and teams. Real Madrid is the biggest team of all, with star players such as Ronaldo, David Beckham, and Zinedine Zidane. F. C. Barcelona is Real's biggest rival.

Bullfighting

Heading for a festival celebration, you are likely to see signs for *Los Toros*. This is the Spanish name for bullfights. Bullfights are often held at the same time as festivals.

At the end of a bullfight, a man called a matador enters the bullring and tries to kill the bull with a sword. Many people around the world think bullfights are cruel. Despite this, they are very popular in Spain, especially in the south and around Madrid.

Spanish football fans travel all over the world to support their world-class national team.

WORD BANK   flamboyant bright and colourful
mournful very sad

Football

Even more popular than bullfighting is football. The atmosphere at matches is great, with fireworks and drummers at big games. It's almost as much fun to watch football in a café, where crowds gather round the television to cheer their team on.

Flamenco

In flamenco every performance tells a story about love, history, or politics. Even the costumes help tell the story. Flamenco women wear **flamboyant** dresses, with tight waists and a full, frilly skirt. Their hair is gathered in a bun low on their necks to make their necks look longer. The whole effect works to make the **silhouette** of the flamenco guitar. Men wear a hat, waistcoat, and high-waisted trousers.

Flamenco

Flamenco music comes originally from Andalucia. Performances usually feature guitar, dancing, and singing. The high, **mournful** singing style reflects the fact that many songs are about suffering and loss. The performers – and sometimes the audience – often clap their hands or click their fingers to provide extra rhythm.

> Flamenco dancers perform with lots of passion, grace, and dignity.

silhouette shape of a person or thing seen against a light background as just a shadowy outline

These are the days when the whole of Spain has a day off. Many of them are Christian holidays. There is usually plenty going on, but most shops are not open.

1 JANUARY – New Year's Day

6 JANUARY – Epiphany, a Christian festival celebrating the baby Jesus

Most regions have holiday days around Easter, but not all regions have the same days (see the sidebar on p. 23 for more holidays).

Time off

Even if you wanted to learn flamenco, it takes years and you don't have time to join a class! So what activities could you take part in right now?

In the south, playing football is one of the most popular sports. Walking and rock climbing are also popular. Each year, more and more people are going mountain biking in the hills, too. Some of the world's best mountain bikers are Spanish.

Spaniards love the sea. You could join them on the beach, for a spot of swimming, sailing, or just plain sunbathing.

Holiday-makers and locals alike enjoy the sun, sea, and sand on the beach at Barcelona.

In the north, road cycling is especially popular. The Basque region is the heartland of Spanish cycling. Driving up a steep mountain you may see names such as "Indurain" or "Mayo" painted in white. These are the great heroes of Spanish cycling. The fans paint their names to encourage the racers in the *Vuelta a España*, or Tour of Spain.

Cinema

If you can speak any Spanish, maybe you could go to see a film. People all over the country love going to the cinema. Luis Buñuel is a famous director from the past. Today, Pedro Almodóvar is world-famous. So are Spanish actors such as Penelope Cruz and Antonio Banderas.

1 MAY – May Day, a spring celebration

15 AUGUST – Assumption Day, another Christian festival

12 OCTOBER – Day of Spain, the national day

6 DECEMBER – Constitution Day, in celebration of Spain's democratic constitution

8 DECEMBER – Day of the Immaculate Conception, a Christian celebration of Jesus's mother, Mary

24 AND 25 DECEMBER – Christmas Eve and Day

◄ The Basque rider Iban Mayo (right) is one of the world's top cyclists. Here he is racing in the *Vuelta a España* in 2002, in which he came in fifth.

Zara takes over!

One of Spain's most successful companies is the fashion chain Zara. Zara has a revolutionary approach to fashion. Store managers report which clothes sell best. They suggest changes, such as different colours. Head office passes the information on to the factories, and the new colours are in the shops 2 or 3 weeks later.

The working day

Of course, while you're here in Spain you won't have to go to school. But while you're having fun exploring, what are ordinary Spanish people up to?

People usually start work at about 9:30 a.m., then stop at 1:30 p.m. They use the hottest part of the day for a **siesta**. Then they start work again at about 4:30 p.m., before finally finishing at about 8 p.m.

Spanish opening hours are slowly changing. Big stores and chains of shops have started to open for more typical European hours, starting at 9 a.m. and finishing at 6 p.m.

Zara's owner is one of Spain's wealthiest men, thanks to the success of his fashion stores around the world.

August holidays

During August, usually the hottest month, many Spanish people take a holiday. The cities seem deserted. Lots of the shops and restaurants close for the whole month. Only the parts of Spain that holidaymakers visit are busy.

School days

Spanish children have to go to school between the ages of six and sixteen. Most have already started school, though. Over 99 per cent of four and five-year-olds go to pre-school. The school day starts at 9 a.m. and finishes at 5 p.m. At midday, children take a 3-hour break – just like almost everyone else. Some head home for a **siesta**, but many kids do sports or play.

These Spanish teenagers socialize in town together at the end of the school day.

Urban Spain

MADRID

You are here!

By now, you've spent enough time in and around Tarifa. It's time to head to the heart of Spain – to the capital city, Madrid.

The city of Algeciras is just along the coast north-east of Tarifa. From here you can catch a train through the hills of Andalucia to Cordoba. From Cordoba, a high-speed train will whisk you to Madrid. On the way, you cross the dusty plains of Castille. This is land the **Moors** and Christians fought over for centuries.

Madrid fact file

FOUNDED AS CAPITAL:
1561, by King Felipe II

POPULATION:
3 million

CITY AREA:
607 square kilometres
(234 square miles)

DISTANCE FROM SEA:
300 kilometres
(186 miles)

**HEIGHT ABOVE
SEA LEVEL:**
650 metres (2,133 feet)

Castille gets its name from the castles that were built there to defend against Moorish attacks.

➤

metro city train, which often runs underground

Finally the train pulls in at the *Estacion de Atocha*, one of Madrid's two main stations. From here you can take the **metro** into the heart of the city.

Puerta del Sol

In the middle of Madrid is the *Puerta del Sol*. This square is also in the middle of Spain. The distance from Madrid to Spain's other big cities is measured from here. On the south side of the square, a stone slab marks the starting-point – *Kilometre Zero*.

Madrid is famous for its art collections and buildings. Like most European capitals, it is crowded with busy traffic and lots of people. The people of Madrid have a reputation for enjoying life. The streets are always busy with people socializing and having a good time.

The Prado

The Prado is one of Madrid's most famous landmarks. It is a museum housing one of the world's oldest art collections. Among the 8,600 paintings here are the works of famous Spanish painters such as Velázquez and Goya.

Santa Eulalia

Santa Eulalia is one of the patron saints of Barcelona. In February the city has a whole week of music and dancing, children's parades, and fireworks to celebrate the saint's special day.

Spanish cities

The *Kilometre Zero* marker in Madrid is where six of Spain's national highways begin. Starting from here, you could head back south towards any of Spain's three "Great Cities" – Granada, Toledo, or Seville. These ancient cities are among the oldest and most beautiful in Spain.

Toledo stands on a rocky mound. The city is cut off on three sides by the **gorge** of the Tajo River. Almost every space has been built on, and churches, **synagogues**, and **mosques** are everywhere.

ATLANTIC OCEAN

Bilbao's Guggenheim Museum (back) is home to many modern, exciting pieces of art. The large puppy-shaped sculpture in the foreground is *Puppy* by the American artist Jeff Koons.

Seville is the greatest city in the south of Spain. It is famous for its architecture, the amazing festivals that are held there, and its bullfights.

WORD BANK   **funicular** railway that climbs up a very steep hill, pulled by cables
gorge steep-sided river valley

Alternatively you could head east to Valencia or Barcelona. Or you could travel north, towards the cities of the Atlantic coast. Which will you pick, and why?

Toledo steel

In the Middle Ages, Toledo was famous for producing high-quality steel, especially swords and daggers. The blades were so good that some are even said to have found their way to Japan!

Bilbao is famous for its Guggenheim Museum, an amazing silver art gallery that gleams in the sun. It is an old industrial city, one of the wealthiest in Spain. Visitors can catch a **funicular** train up into the hills above Bilbao for a view of the whole city.

There is plenty to see in Barcelona! The buildings of the famous architect Gaudi, the city's beaches, the world-famous Ramblas shopping district, and, of course, the festivals all attract visitors.

FRANCE

- Bilbao
- Barcelona

SPAIN

- Madrid
- Toledo
- Valencia
- Minorca
- Palma de Majorca
- Ibiza

PORTUGAL

MEDITERRANEAN SEA

- Seville
- Granada

MOROCCO

The ancient city of Toledo has now been classified as a Spanish National Monument.

Valencia is one of Spain's most modern cities, and its third biggest. Recently a new **metro** system and a centre for **culture** have been built. Like Seville, Valencia is famous for its many festivals.

mosque place of worship for Muslims
synagogue place of worship for Jews

Growth of the cities

Over the years, more and more Spaniards have moved to live in the cities:

1950 60 percent of the population lives in cities

1970 66 percent of the population lives in cities

2000 78 percent of the population lives in cities

Urban life

In the past, most Spaniards lived in the countryside. They worked on the land, growing crops to eat and sell. Today, though, most Spanish people live in cities and towns. By the year 2000, 78 percent of Spaniards lived in **urban** areas.

City problems

Spain's big cities suffer from the same problems as cities everywhere. The streets are often clogged with cars, which causes air **pollution**. Living space is cramped. An average-sized Spanish apartment would seem small to many people from the United States or Australia, for example.

This is Madrid – the huge, crowded capital city of Spain.

WORD BANK   **pollution** release of harmful chemicals and other substances into the air, water, and soil

City bonuses

So why do people move to the cities? One big reason is for work. Most jobs are based in cities. There are more chances to find work, whether you want to work in computers, a restaurant, a shop, or a factory.

Spanish people of all ages enjoy city life because it is so busy. There is always someone to talk to or something to do. There are thousands of restaurants, theatres, art galleries, parks, sports centres, and other attractions.

Many young Spanish people have moved to the cities from the countryside. They spend a lot of time out and about, making the cities lively, exciting places.

Europe's happiest cities!

According to a report in 2001, Spanish cities are the happiest in Europe with few reported cases of **depression**:

Country	Urban population with depression
Spain	2.6 percent
Ireland	12.8 percent
UK	17.1 percent

People enjoy the evening sun at a lively outdoor café in the city of Barcelona.

urban to do with a city or town

Transport

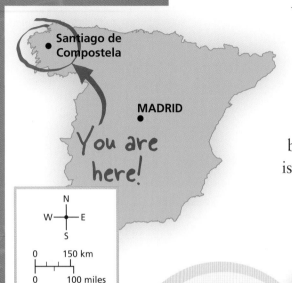

You have left Madrid and are heading for Santiago de Compostela. You need to get to the town in time for a special festival on 25 July – the *Dia de Santiago*, or Day of Saint James. Saint James is the **patron saint** of Spain. Santiago is where Saint James's bones are supposed to be buried. The *Dia* is the biggest festival in this part of Spain.

Thousands of people take part in the festival of Saint James in Santiago, which ends with a fantastic firework display. ▶

The pilgrim trail

For centuries, Christian **pilgrims** have walked to Santiago from other parts of Europe. They come to visit the remains of Saint James, which are said to lie in the cathedral. Making the journey was said to wipe away half of the bad deeds pilgrims had committed in their lives.

Getting around in Spain

The quickest way to Santiago is to fly. There are small airports all over Spain, and flying to Santiago from Madrid will take you just over an hour.

Going by train can be almost as quick as flying. Spain is linked into Europe's high-speed inter-city train network, which can whizz you from Madrid to Paris, France, in just a few hours. Local trains are slower because they stop at tiny villages.

As well as good air and train systems, Spain has excellent roads. A system of motorways links the cities together. Smaller roads connect the towns and villages.

Millions of tourists visit Spain each year by plane. The busiest airports are in the south, where visitors are attracted by the warm weather.

Rural life

Santiago is in the region of Spain called Galicia. This is one of the most **rural** parts of Spain. As you explore the countryside, you see that the land is divided into small plots. The people grow grapes as well as cabbages, turnips, and other vegetables. In the past, women usually worked in the fields. The men spent their time out on the sea fishing.

Galicia is one of Spain's poorest regions. For hundreds of years people have been leaving to look for better-paid work elsewhere. Recently, this has happened in other parts of Spain, too. Young people leave the villages to look for work in the cities.

Languages of Spain

Not everyone in Spain speaks Spanish as his or her main language. Many of the people who speak another language live in rural areas:

Language	Percentage of speakers:
Spanish	74 percent
Catalan	17 percent
Galician	7 percent
Basque	2 percent

Many young people have moved to the cities for work. This often leaves mainly older people living in Spain's villages.

- Nc balancegeu les cistelles.
- No balancear las cestas.

Heu de sortir de l'atracció abans de tornar-la a utilitzar.

Deben abandonar la atracción antes (repetir su utilizaci

Mínim 2 persone

Mínimo 2 personas.

Some regions of Spain are determined to preserve their own languages. This sign, for a ride at a funfair, is in both Basque and Spanish.

Buyers from abroad

People from abroad have started buying homes in rural Spain. In the 1980s, house prices were very low. Most Spanish people were moving to the cities. Few people wanted houses in the country.

Today, there are so many wealthier buyers from abroad that prices have gone up. The foreigners often pay local people to do work such as building or cleaning. This brings employment to the area. But the new, higher house prices mean that it is sometimes difficult for local people to buy homes for themselves.

Offshore Spain

The Balearic Islands in the Mediterranean Sea and the Canary Islands in the Atlantic Ocean, off the coast of Morocco, are especially popular with holidaymakers and people who want to buy homes abroad.

A possible buyer searches for the best deal on a Spanish house.

Farming

Travelling through the countryside of north-western Galicia is like stepping back in time. The land is divided into such small fields that machinery cannot be used on it. People use simple ploughs or dig the soil by hand. You might even see an ox cart with solid wooden wheels, being used to move crops.

Galicia
MADRID
You are here!
N
W
E
S
0
150 km
0
100 miles

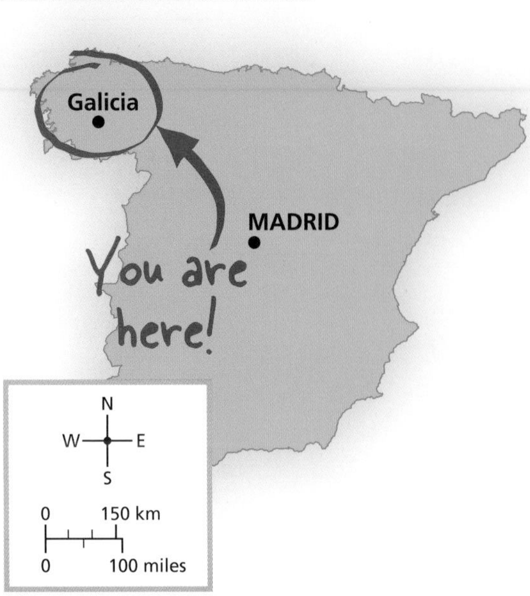

Gallegos in Argentina

Galicia is so poor that many Gallegos (people from Galicia) have moved abroad in search of a better life. Many went to Argentina in South America. Some people joke that there are now more Gallegos in Buenos Aires (Argentina's capital) than in Galicia!

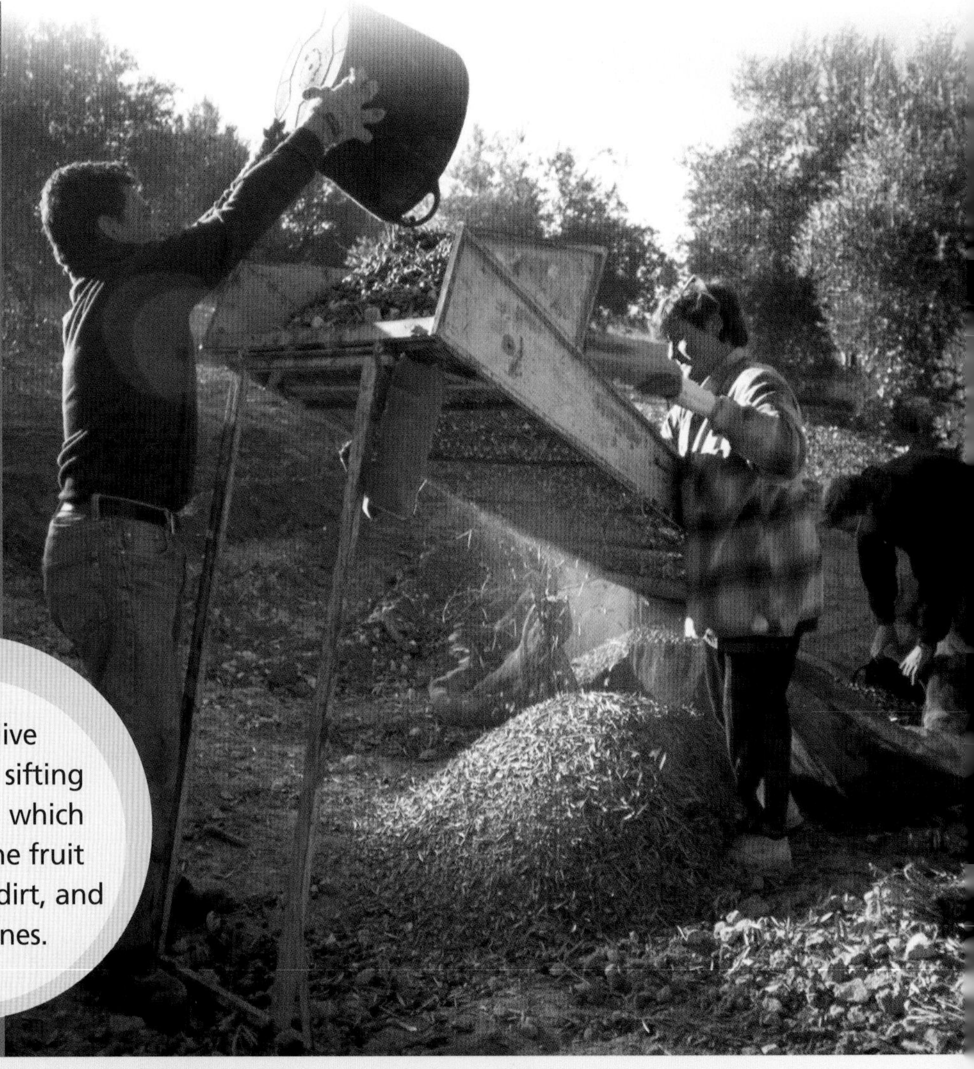

These olive farmers are sifting the harvest, which separates the fruit from leaves, dirt, and small stones.

 WORD BANK **export** send to a foreign country to be sold

One of the most prized animal crops is beef. If you are not a vegetarian, you might like to try a local *churrasqueirá*. These are places where you can buy a huge grilled beefsteak. Often it is flavoured with a sauce called *salsa picante*. Be careful if you try some of this – it's very spicy!

Elsewhere in Spain, many crops are grown for **export**. Spain's warm winter weather means it can grow foods that colder countries only grow in summer. Tomatoes, lettuce, apples, oranges, and all sorts of fruit and vegetables are grown. These are then loaded on to lorries and transported north, to countries such as the UK, France, and Germany.

Spanish farms vary in size. At one extreme are small farmers like those in Galicia. Small farmers often have a mix of crops – some cattle or sheep, olive trees, and a few vegetable crops. Bigger farms specialize in one crop, such as tobacco or wheat.

Horreos

Travellers often notice these strange buildings dotted across the Galician countryside. A *horreo* is a typical local grain store. They are made of hard granite rock and stand on pillars. The granite and pillars keep out rats and damp.

Disappearing cod

Cod, one of the world's most popular types of fish for eating, is slowly disappearing from the seas because so many have been caught. The Grand Banks **fishery**, off Newfoundland, Canada, has now been closed to commercial fishing. People hope that this will help the cod numbers recover, but it is bad news for Basques who make their living by fishing.

Fishing

Travelling along the coast of Galicia can be very time-consuming! This is because all along the coast are steep-sided **inlets**. These are called *rías*. The *rías* are rich fishing grounds, and there are fleets of small boats in most waterside towns.

Further along the north coast, the Basque people were famous whalers and cod fishermen for hundreds of years. The Basques are even said to have reached North America centuries before Columbus. They were chasing the cod catch, and discovered the rich fishing areas off the coast of Newfoundland, Canada. The Basques kept their discovery secret because they did not want other fishermen to follow them.

Mussels are a popular food in Spain. In Galicia mussels were traditionally grown on *mejilloneiras*, rafts like the ones shown here.

fishery area where fish are often caught

People throughout Spain love to eat fish. Even far from the sea, restaurants serve fresh fish on most days. Because fish is such a popular food, fishing is important along all the coasts of Spain. Spain's fishing fleet is one of the world's largest. In the Mediterranean Sea the catches are smaller, but the demand for fish is still high.

Salt cod with cream

This Spanish recipe comes from 1730:

1 Put flakes of boiled salt cod in a saucepan with cream.

2 Add pepper and a handful of parsley.

3 Melt in some butter and the yolks of two or three eggs.

4 Dish it up, and add a poached egg and sliced lemon on top.

◄ These weird-looking flattened bits of fish are salt cod. Salt cod is a great favourite in Spain, as well as many other countries that border the Atlantic Ocean.

inlet where the coastline goes inland

Tourism & travel

While out for the evening *paseo* in Santiago, you meet someone your own age. Not only does your new friend speak good English, their dad is a pilot. He has flown all over Spain, and offers to make a list of places you might like to visit.

Guggenheim Museum, Bilbao

The Guggenheim Museum is one of Spain's most amazing buildings, opened in 1997. The silver plates on the sides of the Guggenheim Museum are meant to look like the scales of a carp fish. While you're here, visit the *Casco Viejo*, the oldest part of the city.

Montfragüe Natural Park

The Montfragüe Natural Park in the Extremadura region has one of the driest, rockiest landscapes in Spain. The park is famous for its birds of prey, especially eagles and vultures.

The Guggenheim Museum was designed by American architect Frank Gehry. It attracts tens of thousands of visitors each year.

The Grand Mosque, Cordoba

The biggest and most beautiful **mosque** is the Grand Mosque, built by the **Moors**. After visiting it, explore the city's cathedral or go down to the river to see the Roman bridge or the Moorish waterwheels.

Castles of Castille

The landscape south of Madrid is dotted with castles built to defend the area against the Moors. Many are open to visitors.

Balearic Islands

Mallorca, Menorca, Ibiza and Formentera, off the east coast of Spain, are full of tourists in the summer due to the hot weather and great nightlife. The best time to explore the Balearic islands is in spring or autumn, when the weather is still warm, but the crowds have gone.

Mount Teide

Visit Mount Teide on the Canary island of Tenerife. It is Spain's highest mountain at 3,718 metres (12,198 feet). At the top is a famous **observatory**.

The Grand Mosque is said to house a bone from the arm of Mohammed, the founder of the Muslim religion.

The stars can be seen especially clearly from the observatory on Mount Teide in the Canary Islands. It is high up, and there are no big cities nearby to light up the night sky.

Stay, or go home?

So, you've been to Andalucia, crossed the whole of Spain from south to north, visited Madrid, heard about the festivals, and seen the **pilgrims** on their way to Santiago. You've even gotten used to having an afternoon **siesta!**

There is still plenty more to see and do. What will you do next? Head for home – or explore more of this exciting country?

- **Watch the bull run in San Fermin, Pamplona**
  A major part of the Fiesta de San Fermin is the bull run. They charge through the narrow streets as brave competitors run ahead of them. It is a dangerous activity, and every year people are hurt by the bulls.

- **Go celebrity spotting in Mallorca**
  As well as holiday crowds, the island is home to world-famous celebrities such as the supermodel Claudia Schiffer.

- **Go skiing or snowboarding in the Sierra Nevada**
  One of Europe's southern-most ski resorts is at *Sol y Nieve* (Sun and Snow).

- **Take part in *Semana Santa***
  The Easter-week **processions**, *Semana Santa*, in Seville and Malaga are famous throughout Spain. But almost every town and village has its own Easter festival.

- **Visit the aqueduct at Segovia**
  2,000 years old and around 800 metres (2,625 feet) long, this aqueduct was built by the Romans.

- **Go shopping at the *Rastro* in Madrid**
  The *Rastro* is a market held in Madrid every Sunday. People go to hunt for second-hand bargains, but also to meet their friends and chat.

- **Go to the Feria de Abril**
  This is a week-long festival in Seville, featuring horse riders in costumes, dance tents with flamenco performances, and daily bullfights.

- **Watch the Mundaka Pro**
  This world-famous surfing contest is held at Mundaka in northern Spain in October. Huge crowds gather to watch the surfers ride some of Europe's best waves.

Find out more

World Wide Web

If you want to find out more about Spain, you can search the Internet using keywords such as these:

- Spain
- River Ebro
- The European Union

You can also find your own keywords by using headings or words from this book. Try using a search directory such as **www.yahooligans.com**.

Movies

The Mask of Zorro (1998)
It's the early 1800s. An aging Zorro, Don Diego de la Vega, is imprisoned just as Spain loses California to General Santa Anna. He escapes from prison and trains a new Zorro to take his place in the fight against his enemy, Montero.

Belle Epoque (1992)
A young soldier deserts from the army and goes to a country farm, where he is welcomed by the owner and his daughters. Problems arise when the soldier falls in love with all four daughters.

Are there ways for an eager Destination Detective to find out more about Spain? Luckily, yes! There are books, websites, and addresses to write to for more information:

The Spanish Embassy

The Spanish Embassy in your own country can give you lots of information about Spain. They can tell you about the different regions, times of the year for travelling, special events, and Spanish culture. Many embassies also have their own website. In the UK you can write to:

The Spanish Embassy
39 Chesham Place
London
SW1X 8SB.

Details of other Spanish embassies, as well as some basic facts about Spain's different regions, can be found at **www.spain.embassyhomepage.com**

Further reading

The following books are full of information about Spain:

Pick Your Brains About Spain, Mandy Kirkby (Cadogan Guides, 2004)

Take Your Camera: Spain, Ted Park (Raintree, 2004)

The Rough Guide To Spain (Rough Guides, 2004)

World of Recipes: Spain, Su Townsend and Caroline Young (Heinemann Library, 2004)

Timeline

1000 BC
The Phoenicians begin to colonize Spain.

400 BC
The Carthaginians conquer much of Spain.

200 BC
The Romans drive the Carthaginians from Spain.

AD 400s
The Visigoths capture Spain from the Romans.

711–718
Moorish Muslims conquer almost all of Spain.

1000s
Christian kingdoms in the north begin their attempt to drive the Muslims from Spain.

1479
The kingdoms of Aragon and Castile unite, bringing almost all of what is now Spain under one rule.

1492
Spanish forces conquer Granada, the last centre of Muslim control in Spain. Christopher Columbus sails to the Americas and claims them for Spain.

1512
King Ferdinand V seizes the Kingdom of Navarre, completing the unification of what is now Spain.

1556–1598
The Spanish **empire** reaches its greatest power during the reign of Philip II.
In 1588 the English navy defeats the Spanish Armada.

1808
The invading French armies of Napoleon Bonaparte seize Madrid.

1808–1814
Spanish, Portuguese, and English forces, commanded by the Duke of Wellington, slowly drive the French from Spain.

1810–1825
All of Spain's American colonies, except Cuba and Puerto Rico, revolt and declare their **independence**. By this time, Spain had lost almost all its empire.

1898
Spain loses control of Cuba, Puerto Rico, and the Philippines in a war with the United States.

1931
King Alfonso XIII leaves Spain, which becomes a democratic republic.

1936–1939
The Spanish **Civil War** between Nationalists led by General Francisco Franco and the Republicans begins in 1936. In 1939, Franco becomes the ruler of Spain.

1975
Franco dies. Spaniards begin setting up a new, democratic government.

1978
Spaniards approve a new Constitution based on democratic principles.

1981
Colonel Antonio Tejero launches an attempt to take over the government by the army. It fails when most army officers do not support him.

1986
Spain joins the European Community, an economic organization that became the European Union in 1993.

Spain – facts & figures

The Spanish flag has three horizontal stripes. The top and bottom stripes are equal-sized and red, while the middle yellow stripe is double the size of the red stripes. The national coat of arms can be on the yellow band. There is also a civil flag of Spain, which does not have the coat of arms on it (seen here).

People and places

- Population: 42.7 million.
- Over 800 million people worldwide speak Spanish.
- Average life expectancy: 78.1 years

Money matters

- Before converting to the euro in 2002, Spain's currency was the peseta, made up of 100 duros.
- Average earnings:
Men – £15,680 (US$27,503)
Women – £6,722.40 (US$11,791)

What's in a name?

- Spain's official name is Reino de España, or Regne d'Espanya, in Catalan, and Espainiako Erresuma in Basque.

Food facts

- The Spanish brought chocolate to Europe from Mexico.
- The potato had been growing in Bolivia and Peru for hundreds of years, but the Spanish conquistadors discovered it in 1537 and introduced it to the rest of the world.

Glossary

arable farmland where crops are grown

border imaginary line dividing one country from another

civil war war between groups from within the same country. In Spain, the civil war was between the Nationalists and the Republicans.

culture art, music, and theatre

depression general feeling of sadness and lack of hope

empire groups of countries controlled by one country

export sale in a foreign country

fishery area where fish are often caught

flamboyant bright and colourful

funicular railway that climbs up a very steep hill, pulled by cables

gorge steep-sided river valley

independence when an area governs itself. Several regions of Spain have political parties campaigning for independence, including the Basque region and Catalunya.

inlet where the coastline goes inland

legacy something handed down through time

looted stolen during a battle or riot

metro city train, which often runs underground

mosque place of worship for Muslims

mournful very sad

muezzin official at a mosque who calls Muslims to prayer

observatory place for studying the night sky, usually through telescopes

parliament group of people elected to make laws

patron saint religious figure associated with a place, country, job, or institution

pilgrim person making a religious journey

plateau high area of flat land

procession group of people moving in a line as part of a celebration. During festivals processions often end at the church.

pollution release of harmful chemicals and other substances into the air, water, and soil

rural to do with the countryside

siege when a building is surrounded by enemy forces who stop anyone arriving or leaving

siesta short nap, especially in hot countries when the sun gets very hot in the afternoon

silhouette shape of a person or thing seen against a light background as just a shadowy outline

synagogue place of worship for Jews

territory area of land

urban to do with a city or town

Index